Black & White Photographs
original images

Joseph Fleming

Colorblind Fine Art

Decades of being around accomplished talent producing absolutely phenomenal quality work has taught that we are capable of greatness. It is possible to meet our destiny and become it. Experiencing excellence done with such apparent ease and humble selfless gratification is the motivation for this photography. Most important was having the freedom.

Being colorblind gives an advantage when composing black & white… less confusion.
This special collection selected from thousands of captures. All images were framed
in the camera and presented without edits, genuine as seen through the lens.
Panchromatic conversion applied by unique proprietary process.

Limited prints and custom work available.

info@ BEACHNOISE.com

JOSEPH FLEMING

0125

0440

0471

0705

0780

0826

0920

1173

1581

1608

1976

2121

2180

2397

2467

2686

2688

2962

3147

3151

3359

3621

3656

3714

3752

3778

3795

3937

4035

4070

4099

4128

4193

5492

5497

5750

5784

5811

6095

6176

7182

8407

8470

8815

8896

9024

9353

9430

9970

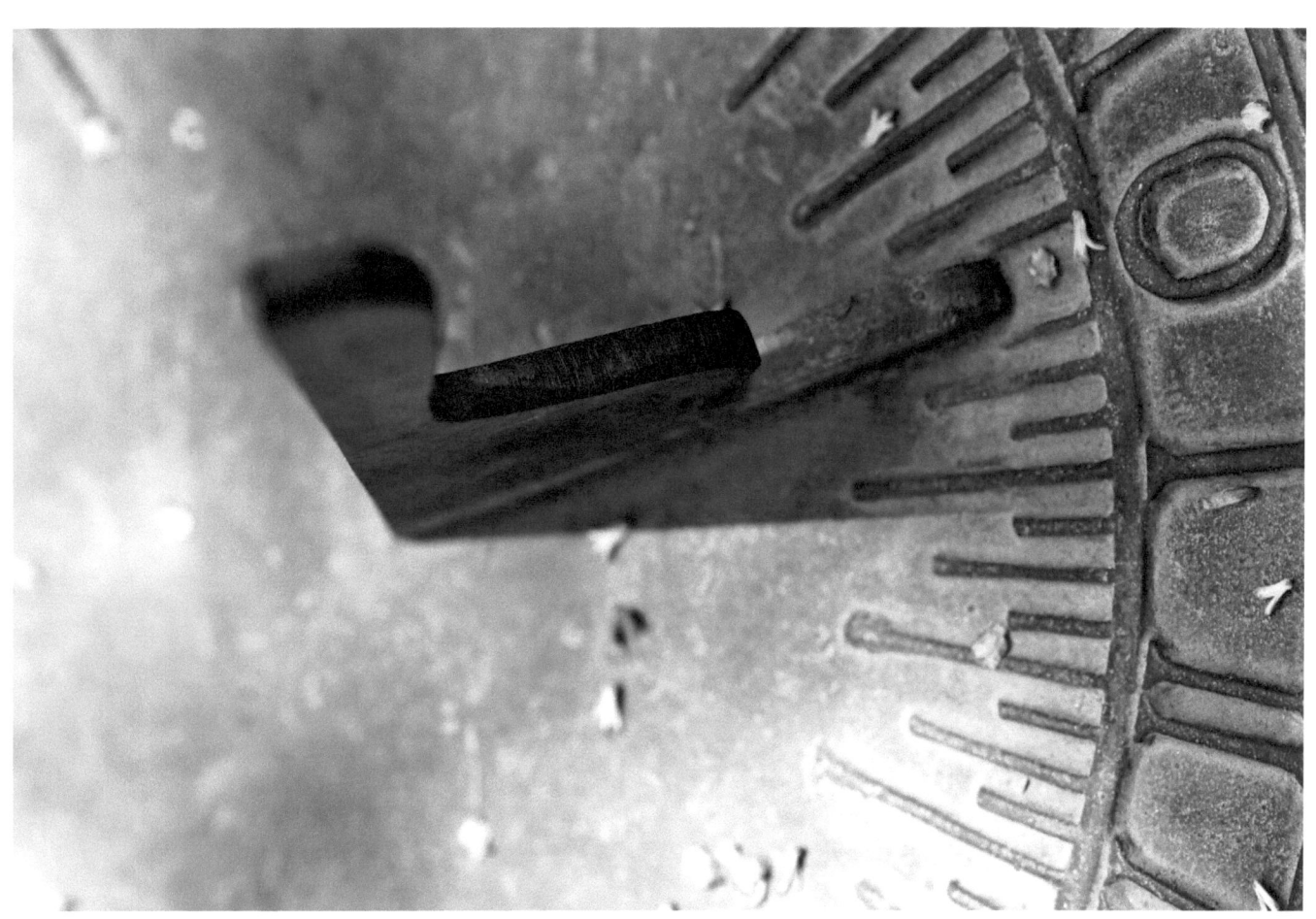

10002

www.ingramcontent.com/pod-product-compliance
Lightning Source LLC
Chambersburg PA
CBHW050814180526
45159CB00004B/1663